Yoga for Youngsters

[playful poses for little people]

Kat Randall

While enjoying this book with
your youngsters, encourage them to:

Breathe.

Remember to inhale and exhale.

Alliterate.

Notice words having the same first sound.

Affirm.

Affirmations are great things you say to yourself.

Speak Spanish.

Notice the Spanish translations.

Have fun!

I am **f**riendly
like a **f**lamingo.

flamingo

flamingo pose

I am **e**xtraordinary like an **e**agle.

águila

eagle pose

I am **t**errific like a **t**ree.

árbol

tree pose

I am **l**oveable
like a **l**ion.

león

lion pose

I am **s**mart
like a **s**nake.

vibora

snake pose

I am **b**eautiful like a **b**utterfly.

mariposa

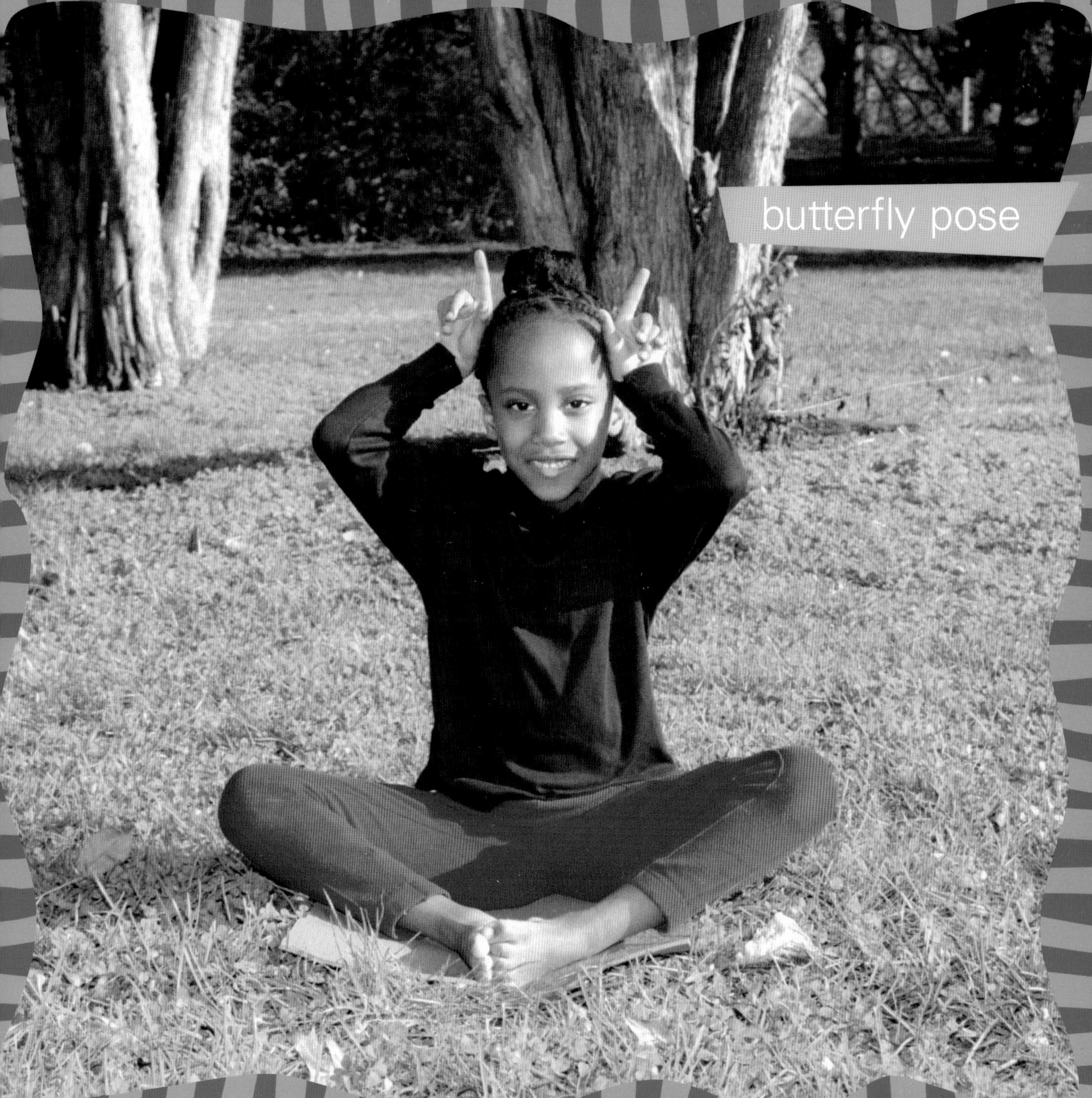
butterfly pose

I am **t**alented
like a **t**urtle.

tortuga

turtle pose

I am **c**alm
like a **c**amel.

camello

camel pose

I am **c**reative like a **c**andle.

vela

candle pose

I am **p**owerfully **p**eaceful.

tigre

shava-asana

To order more copies of this book:

e-mail akatskidskreation@hotmail.com
fax 314-963-0494
web www.akatskidskreation.com

Cost: $12.95 plus tax & shipping

A grateful gracias:

• To the yoga youngsters: Buck, Bonnie, Helen, Ebura, Dominic, Nick, Lucy, Marlon, Michelle and Paige.

• To Esperanza, my amiga.

Some of my favorite resources:

YogaKids: Educating the Whole Child Through Yoga, Marsha Wenig (Stewart, Tabori & Chang, 2003) Interested in training? Go to www.yogakids.com.

Fly Like a Butterfly, Shakta Kaur Khalsa (Rudra Press 1998)

Children's Book of Yoga: Games & Exercises Mimic Plants & Animals & Objects, Thia Luby. (Clear Light Publishers, 1998)

Spinning Inward: Using Guided Imagery with Children for Learning, Creativity & Relaxation, Maureen Murdock. (Shambhala Publications, 1988)

Yoga for Children, Mary Stewart & Kathy Phillips (Fireside, 1993)

Yoga for Children, Swati and Rajiv Chanchani. (UBS Publishers' Distributors Ltd., 1995)

Yoga and The Special Child: A Therapeutic Approach for Infants and Children with Down Syndrome, Cerebral Palsy, and Learning Disabilities, Sonia Sumar. (Special Yoga Publishers, 1998)

Yoga with Kids - Complete Idiot's Guide, Jodi B. Komitor & Eve Adamson

Yoga, The Spirit and Practice of Moving into Stillness, Erich Schiffmann (Simon & Schuster, Inc., 1996)